The Funniest Chicago Bears Joke Book Ever

Copyright

Version 1

This book is a joke book, written in a light hearted way.

No offence is meant to any person or group of people

Read, laugh and enjoy a joke

Introduction

Thank you for taking the time to read "The Funniest Chicago Bears Joke Book Ever". In this book we take a light hearted look at football and our rivals.

We have scoured the country for some of the best and funniest jokes, most jokes were thought up at the stadium or in the bar after a game and a few beers.

This book covers some of the best jokes; no joke has been kept out of this book for being politically incorrect or too rude.

Get ready to share a laugh at our rival's expense …

St. Peter was manning the Pearly Gates when 40 Green Bay fans showed up. Never having seen a Packers fan at heaven's door, St. Peter said he would have to check with God. After hearing the news, God instructed him to admit the 10 most virtuous from the group.

A few minutes later, Saint Peter returned to God breathless and said, "They're gone."
"What? All of the Packers fans are gone?" asked God.
"No" replied Saint Peter "The Pearly Gates!"

What is the difference between Packers fan and a coconut?

One's thick and hairy and the others a tropical fruit

Three old football fans are in a church, praying for their teams.

The first one asks, "Oh lord, when will we get to the Super Bowl?" God replies "In two years' time"
"But I will be dead by then", said the old man.

The second fan asks "When will we next win the Super Bowl?"
"In ten years' time", God replies
But I'll be dead by then, said the old man

The last man asks "When will the Packers win the Super Bowl?"

God thinks and then says "I will be dead by then"

Rumor has it that to cut the cost of the repairs to the Vikings scoreboard, only the light bulbs in the half used to show the opponents score will be fixed.

The other half will just have 'Minnesota Vikings 0' painted on in yellow paint.

The Vikings are apparently under investigation by the IRS for tax evasion; they've been claiming for Silver Polish for the past 10 years.

Q. What's the difference between a female Packers fan and a pit bull?

A. Lipstick

There was once a fanatical Bears fan who thought of nothing but football all day long. He talked about football, read about football, watched nothing but football on television and attended games as often as he possibly could.

Finally his poor wife could not stand it any longer. One night she said, 'I honestly believe you love the Bears more than you love me!'

'Gosh,' said the fan, 'I love the Steelers more than I love you!'

I've started watching the Vikings, as my doctor says I should avoid any excitement.

Top tip for Cowboys fans: don't waste money on expensive new jerseys every season.

Simply strap a large inflatable penis to your forehead, and everyone will immediately know which team you support.

One of the highest paid players in the NFL, John had everything going for him. He had an expensive new mansion, a new sports car, a wardrobe full of designer clothes.

His only problem was that he had three girlfriends and he couldn't decide which one to marry. So he decided to give $5,000 to each woman to see what she would do with it.

The first woman bought new clothes for herself and had an expensive new hairdo, a massage, facial, manicure and pedicure.

The second woman bought a top-of-the range DVD and CD player, as well as an expensive set of golf clubs and tennis racquet and gave them all to John. "I used the money to buy you these gifts because I love you," she told him.

The third woman invested the money in the stock market, and within a short time had doubled her investment. She gave John back the initial $5,000 and reinvested the profit. "I'm investing in our future because I love you so much," she said.

John considered carefully how each woman had spent the money, and then married the woman with the biggest breasts.

A quarterback had had a particularly bad season and announced that he was retiring from professional football. In a television interview he was asked his reasons for quitting the game.

'Well, basically,' he said, 'it's a question of illness and fatigue.'

'Can you be more specific?' asked the interviewer.

'Well,' said the player, 'specifically the fans are sick and tired of me.

A woman goes to see the doctor.
"Doctor, doctor, I'm very worried about my son," she said. "All he does is play football all day; then he comes in covered in mud and walks all over my clean carpet."

"I think you may be over-reacting," said the doctor reassuringly. "Sons often behave like that"

"I know, doctor," said the woman, "but it's not just me that's worried about him. His wife is too"

My wife told me last week that she'd leave me if I didn't stop spending so much time at football games.

'What a shame!'

'Yes. I shall miss her'

A woman was reading a newspaper one morning and said to her husband,

'Look at this, dear. There's an article here about a man who traded his wife for a season ticket to the Bears. You wouldn't do a thing like that, would you?'

'Of course I wouldn't!' replied her husband. 'The season's almost over!'

Snow White arrived home one evening to find her home destroyed by fire. She was especially worried because she'd left all seven dwarves asleep inside. As she scrambled among the wreckage, frantically calling their names, suddenly she heard the cry: " The Packers for the Super Bowl."

"Thank goodness," sobbed Snow White. "At least Dopey's still alive!"

The ASPCA have acted swiftly after recent results.

If you see any Green Bay fans walking a dog please call them immediately on 6-0, 6-6 6-12 6-18 6-24 as they're not very good at holding on to leads

Four surgeons are taking a coffee break:

1st surgeon says "Accountants are the best to operate on because when you open them up, everything inside is numbered"

2nd surgeon says "Nope, librarians are the best. Everything inside them is in alphabetical order"

3rd surgeon says "Well you should try electricians. Everything inside them is color coded"

4th surgeon says "I prefer Packers fans. They're heartless, spineless, gutless and their heads and butts are interchangeable"

Q. How do you change a Packers fans mind?

A. Blow in his ear!

Q. What's the difference between a Packers fan and a broken clock?

A. Even a broken clock is right twice a day

Q. What's the difference between a Vikings fan and a coconut?

A. You can get a drink out of a coconut

Two guys were walking through a cemetery when they see a tombstone that read: "Here lies John Smith, a good man and a Packers fan"

So, one of them asked the other: "When the hell did they start putting two people in one grave?"

Two Packers fans jump off a cliff. Which one hits the ground first?

Who gives a F**k!

What do you get when you cross a Packers fan with a pig?

I don't know, there are some things a pig just won't do

Q. What do you call a Packers fan on the moon?

A. A Problem

Q. What do you call 100 Packers fans on the moon?

A. An even bigger problem

Q. What do you call all the Packers fans on the moon?

A. Problem solved

Q. How do you define 199 Viking fans

A. Gross Stupidity

Q. Why do Packers fans whistle whilst sitting on the john?

A. So they know which end to wipe

Q. What's the difference between a Packers fan and an Onion?

A. No one cries when you chop up a Packers fan!

Q. Did you hear that the postal service just recalled their latest stamps?

A. They had photos of Packers players on them, people couldn't figure out which side to spit on

Q. How many Packers fans does it take to pave a driveway?

A. Depends how thin you slice them

Q. What would you call a pregnant Packers fan?

A. A dope carrier

Q. What do you call a Vikings fan with half a brain?

A. Gifted

Q. What do Packers fans use as birth control?

A. Their personalities

Q. How many Vikings supporters does it take to stop a moving Bus?

A. Never enough

Q. What do you call a Packers fan with no arms and legs?

A. Trustworthy

Q. What's the difference between a dead dog in the road and a dead Packers fan?

A. Skid marks in front of the dog

Q. What's the difference between a Packers fan and a Vibrator?

A. A Packers fan is a real dick

Q. If you see a Packers fan on a bicycle, why should you never swerve and hit him?

A. You don't want to damage your bike

Q. What would you call two Packers fans going over a cliff in an SUV?

A. A complete waste of space. You could have squeezed six of them into one of those

Q. What's the difference between a Packers fan and a bucket of crap?

A. The bucket

Q. How do you get a one armed Packers fan down from a tree?

A. Wave at him

Q. How do you keep a Packers
fan busy?

A. Put him in a round room and
tell him to sit in the corner

Q. What do Packers fans and mushrooms have in common?

A. They both sit in the dark and feed on nothing but crap

Q. How many Packers fans does it take to change a light bulb?

A. It doesn't matter, because they're all condemned to eternal darkness

Mike McCarthy was going to the Green Bay Packers Halloween party dressed as a pumpkin

But at midnight he still hadn't turned into a coach

Q. How is a pint of milk different than a Packers fan?

A. If you leave the milk out for a week it develops a culture

Q. What's the difference between a Packers fan and a sperm?

A. At least a sperm has one chance in 5 million of becoming a human being

There's a rumor going about that if you buy a season ticket at Lambeau Field then you get a free space suit.

Apparently it's due to the lack of atmosphere

Q. How do you save a Packers fan from drowning?

A. Take your foot off his head

Q. What's the difference between a busload of Packers fans and a Hedgehog?

A. On a hedgehog, the pricks are on the outside

Q. What do Hemorrhoids and Packers fans have in common?

A. They're both a complete pain in the ass and never seem to go away completely

Q. Why did the Lions fan climb the glass window?

A. To see what was on the other side

Q. What's the difference between a Vikings fan and a Chimp?

A. One's hairy, stupid and smells, and the other is a chimpanzee

An anxious woman goes to her doctor. "Doctor," she asks nervously, "I'm a bit worried - can you get pregnant from anal intercourse?"

"Of course," replies the doctor, "Where do you think Packers fans come from?"

Q. How do you kill a Vikings fan when he's been drinking?

A. Slam the toilet seat on his head

Q. What's the difference between Pamela Anderson and the Packers line?

A. Pam's only got two tits in front of her

Q. Santa Claus, the tooth fairy, an intelligent Packers supporter and an old bum are walking down the street together when simultaneously they each spot a fifty dollar bill. Who gets it?

A. The old bum, of course - the other three are mythical creatures

Q. How can you tell a level headed Vikings fan?

A. He dribbles from both sides of his mouth - at the same time

Newsflash

Thieves broke into the home of a Packers fan and stole two books.

"The thing that upsets me", he said "is that I hadn't finished coloring them in yet!"

Q. What do you get if you cross a Monkey with a Packers fan?

A. Nothing. Monkeys are far too clever to screw a Packers fan

Q. What is the difference between a battery and a Vikings fan?

A. A battery has a positive side

What's the difference between the Vikings defense and a taxi driver?

A taxi driver will only let in four at a time

Q. What do Packers fans and laxatives have in common?

A. They both irritate the crap out of you

Q. What's the ideal weight for a Packers fan?

A. Three pounds, that's including the Urn

Two Packers fans are on the plane on the way to a game

One turns to the other and says "Hey John! If this plane turns upside-down will we fall out?"

"No way Steve," says his friend "of course we'll still be pals!"

Q. You're trapped in a room with a Lion, a snake and a Vikings fan. You have a gun with two bullets. What should you do?

A. Shoot the Vikings fan, twice

Q. What do you call a Packers fan in a suit?

A. The accused

Q. Why did God make Packers fans smelly?

A. So blind people could laugh at them too

Q. What do you call 100 Packers fans at the bottom of a cliff?

A. A good start

Q. What do you call a dead Vikings fan in a closet?

A. Last year's winner of the hide and seek contest

Q. What do you call a Vikings fan that does well on an IQ test?

A. A cheat

Q. What has 120,000 arms and an IQ of 170

A. Lambeau Field during every game

Q. Why do people take an instant dislike to Packers fans?

A. It saves time

Q. What do you say to a Vikings fan with a job?

A. Can I have a Big Mac please

Q. What do you get if you see a Vikings fan buried up to his neck in sand?

A. More sand

Q. What's the difference between a Packers fan and a shopping cart?

A. The cart has a mind of its own

A Packers fan goes to his doctor to find out what's wrong with him.

"Your problem is you're fat" says the doctor

"I'd like a second opinion" responds the man

"OK, you're ugly too" replies the doctor

A Bears and Packers fan get into a nasty car accident. Both vehicles are really wrecked, but amazingly neither of them are hurt.

After they crawl out of their cars, the Bears fan says, "So you're a Packers fan, that's interesting. I'm a Bears fan.

Wow! Just look at our cars. There's nothing left, but fortunately we are unhurt. This must be a sign from God that we should meet and be friends and live together in peace the rest of our days."

The Packers fan replied, "I totally agree, this must be a sign from God!"

The Bears fan went on, "And look at this - here's another miracle. My car is completely demolished but this bottle of Jack Daniels didn't break. Surely God wants us to drink it, to celebrate the fact we are alive?"

He hands the bottle to the Packers fan, who nods his head in agreement, opens it and takes few big swigs from the bottle, then hands it back to the Bears fan.

The Bears fan takes the bottle, immediately puts the cap back on, and hands it back to the Packers fan. The Packers fan asks, "Aren't you having any?"

The Bears fan replies, "Nah ... I think I'll just wait for the cops"

A truck driver used to keep himself amused by scaring every Packers fan he saw walking down the Street in their jersey. He would swerve as if to hit them, and at the last minute, swerve back onto the road.

One day as he was driving along the road, he saw a priest hitch-hiking. He thought he would do his good deed for the day and offer the priest a lift.

"Where are you going, Father?" he asked.

"I'm going to say mass"

"No problem," said the driver, "Jump in and I'll give you a ridc"

The priest climbed into the truck and they set off down the road. Suddenly the driver sees a Packers fan on the sidewalk, and instinctively swerved as if to hit him, but just in time, remembering the priest in his truck, swerved back to the road again, narrowly missing the idiot.

Although he was certain that he didn't hit him, he still heard a loud "Thud". Not understanding where the noise came from, he glanced in his mirrors, and, seeing nothing, said to the priest, "Oh sorry Father, I nearly hit that Packers fan"

"No need to apologize Son," replied Father, "I got the ba*tard with the door!"

Q. What's the difference between OJ Simpson and the Packers?

A. OJ at least had a defense

Q. What do they call a drug ring in Dallas?

A. A huddle

Q. What's the difference between the Green Bay Packers and Cheerios?

A. Cheerios belong in a bowl

Q. Wanna hear a joke?

A. The Green Bay Packers

Q. What's the difference between a vacuum cleaner and the Green Bay Packers?

A. There's only one dirt bag in a vacuum cleaner

Q. What did the Packers fan say after his team won the Super Bowl?

A. "Dammit mom, why'd you wake me up? I was having an amazing dream!"

Q. How are the Packers like my neighbors?

A. They can't pick up a single yard

Q. Want to hear a Packers joke?

A. Ryan Grant

Q. Why is Ryan Grant like a grizzly bear?

A. Every fall he goes into hibernation

Q. What's the difference between the Green Bay Packers and a dollar bill?

A. You can still get four quarters out of a dollar bill

Q. What do the Packers and possums have in common?

A. Both play dead at home and get killed on the road

Q. What is the difference between a Packers fan and a baby?

A. The baby will stop whining after a while

Q. How many Packers players does it take to change a tire?

A. One, unless it's a blowout, in which case they all show up

Q. What do you call 53 millionaires around a TV watching the Super Bowl?

A. The Green Bay Packers

Q. What do the Green Bay Packers and Billy Graham have in common?

A. They both can make 60,000 people stand up and yell "Jesus Christ"

Q. How do you keep a Green Bay player out of your yard?

A. Put up goal posts

Q. Why are so many Green Bay players claiming they have swine flu?

A. So they don't have to touch the pigskin

Q. How do you stop a Green Bay fan from beating his wife?

A. Dress her in a Chicago Bears jersey

Q. If you have a car containing a Packers wide receiver, a Packers linebacker, and a Packers defensive back, who is driving the car?

A. The cop

Q. How do you castrate a Green Bay fan?

A. Kick his sister in the mouth

Q. What should you do if you find three Viking fans buried up to their neck in cement?

A. Get more cement

Q. What's the difference between a Packers fan and a carp?

A. One is a bottom-feeding, scum sucker, and the other is a fish

Q. How did the Vikings fan die from drinking milk?

A. The cow fell on him

Q. What does a Packers fan do when his team wins the Super Bowl?

A. He turns off the PlayStation

Q. What do you call a Green
Bay Packer in the Super Bowl?

A. A referee

Q. Did you hear that the Packers doesn't have a website?

A. They can't string three "W's" together

Q. What does a Packer fan and a bottle of beer have in common?

A. They're both empty from the neck up

Q. Why do Packer fans keep their season tickets on their dashboards?

A. So they can park in handicap spaces

Q. How do you keep a Packers fan from masturbating?

A. You paint his dick in Chicago Bears colors and he won't beat it for 4 years

Q. Why do the Packers want to change their name to the Green Bay Tampons?

A. Because they are only good for one period and do not have a second string

Q. What's the difference between the Green Bay Packers and the Taliban?

A. The Taliban has a running game

Q. Where do you go in Green Bay in case of a tornado?

A. Lambeau Field, they never get a touchdown there

Q. Why do ducks fly over Lambeau Field upside down?

A. There's nothing worth craping on

Q. What do you call a Green Bay Packer with a Super Bowl ring?

A. Senior Citizen

Terror Alert

The Green Bay Packers football practice was delayed for nearly three hours yesterday after a player reported finding an unknown white powdery substance on the practice field.

Practice was stopped and the cops and the FBI were called in. After a complete analysis, FBI forensic experts determined that the white substance unknown to these players was in fact the goal line. Practice resumed after Special Agents decided the team was unlikely to encounter the substance again this season.

There's a rumor that after the current sponsorship expires the Vikings have lined up a new sponsor, Tampax

They thought it was an appropriate change as the team is going through a very bad period

Aaron Rodgers just threw his iPhone in frustration but it was intercepted and returned for a touchdown

Q. What Does the Dallas Cowboys and the movie Broke Back Mountain have in common?

A. They both have cowboys that suck

Q. Why is Aaron Rodgers
unable to answer a telephone?

A. He can't find the receiver

Q. Did you know the Cowboys had a 11 and 5 season this year?

A. 11 arrests, 5 convictions

Q. Why doesn't El Paso have a professional football team?

A. Because then Dallas would want one

After the game, Aaron Rodgers threw his helmet towards the sideline in disgust and that too was intercepted

Q: Why was Aaron Rodgers mad when the Packers playbook was stolen?

A: Because he hadn't finished coloring it

Did you hear about the Packer fan that died at a pic cating contest?

The cow kicked him in the head

What do you call a 350 pound Packer fan?

An anorexic

What do you call a beautiful girl in Green Bay?

A tourist